Break The Silence

Break The Silence

Dina Ibrahim

gatekeeper press
Tampa, Florida

The content associated with this book is the sole work and responsibility of the author. Gatekeeper Press had no involvement in the generation of this content.

Break the Silence

Published by Gatekeeper Press
7853 Gunn Hwy., Suite 209
Tampa, FL 33626
www.GatekeeperPress.com

Copyright © 2024 by Dina Ibrahim

All rights reserved. Neither this book, nor any parts within it may be sold or reproduced in any form or by any electronic or mechanical means, including information storage and retrieval systems, without permission in writing from the author. The only exception is by a reviewer, who may quote short excerpts in a review.

Library of Congress Control Number: 2024948146

ISBN (hardcover): 9781662956799
ISBN (paperback): 9781662956805
eISBN: 9781662956812

Table of Contents

Blood Isn't Thicker Than Water — 1
Toxic Household — 2
Drained — 3
Guide Me — 4
Can't Forgive can't Forget — 5
Hurting — 6
My Mother and Her High Hopes — 7
Change — 8
Behind my Mask — 9
The Monsters — 10
How Much Longer — 11
My Voice will Never Matter — 12
No Matter How Long it Takes — 13

Betrayal and Trust — 15
I'm the Type of Person — 16
I'm Used to People Leaving — 17
The World is Fake — 18
Fighting my Battles — 19
Painful Memories — 20
Hopeless — 21

Broken Glass — 23
Hoping — 24
Did you Ever Really Love Me — 25
Unspoken — 26
Hope You're Doing Okay — 27

Loving You	28
Worst Fear	29
Goodbye	30
I See this Girl	31

Home — 33

What is Love	34
If I Had to Speak about Love	35
I'm Falling for You	36
Before You	37
You Healed Me	38
I Love You	39
Happy Valentine's Day	40
I Crave you like a Drug	41
Happy 1 Year Anniversary	42
Like a Rose	43
Lust and Desire	44
Home	45

Writing Poetry — 47
Writing Poetry	48

Acknowledgements — 49

About the Author — 51

**Blood
Isn't
Thicker
Than
Water**

Toxic Household

Why do we call it a home when I feel like I don't belong? Tired of all the screams and problems that goes on.

I'm tired of the sleepless nights and the tears that never seem to stop, wondering if the toxic habits would ever just drop.

I'm so drained and don't know how to keep it together. They say blood is thicker than water, but not every family is forever.

It's like no matter how far I go I can't escape the stress, trying so hard not to give up just so they can see me success.

I hide my tears and pretend that I don't care, but deep down I just want to scream in despair.

How is it even at home I feel alone? My family wonders how my heart turned into stone.

Only God knows what's real in my heart, and he knows that my family is completely tearing me apart.

Drained

Mom, I know you love me it's not a doubt, but what you don't realize is how I feel every time you shout.

And yes, I shout back, but only because you make my voice feel unheard and my feelings under attack,

But if I were to tell you how this family makes me feel, you would just call me selfish, and blame me for how my feelings are unreal.

I try my best to act like I don't care, but if I'm being honest, it feels like I've run out of air.

How can I feel safe when all I feel is drained? My soul is tired and it's hard to maintain.

I don't even call it a home, it's a house I live in, because if it were a home, I shouldn't be feeling what I feel within,

All the screams and all the hate, I can no longer pretend. I know this family is my blood, but they will never be someone I can ever defend.

I'm sorry If I sound selfish in any way, but I'm just trying to explain how I feel every day.

Mom, I know you love me with all your heart, but this toxic love is slowly tearing me apart.

Guide Me

God, I'm trapped in the darkness and can't find the light. I hate what goes through my mind all through the night.

I don't know how much longer I can fight, but I'm trying so hard to make things right.

Lord, I just need someone to hug me tight, I need someone who's willing to stay, so maybe then I can be alright.

Missing the times where I used to be full of excite, now all the pain and tears has made my heart full of fright.

God, I'm wishing upon a star that shines so bright, to give me hope and peace because I'm starting to lose my sight.

Can't Forgive can't Forget

How am I supposed to just forgive, and how am I supposed to forget and start to live?

How am I supposed to respect them when they don't deserve? They left me here bleeding while they sat back and observed.

I'm tired of feeling like I don't belong. Through silent tears and silent screams, I try to be strong,

I should be crying to my family about my friends, not crying to my friends about my family who I should depend.

I'm feeling lost and empty inside. Hard to explain my hurting that I try to hide,

People always say, "Forgive and Forget," but they don't know that they tore the matches and left me burned deeper than a cigarette.

Even though, I don't let my emotions show, don't ever think that eventually I'll move on and just let it go.

Hurting

Remembering every tear I shed, remembering every scar that spread,

Remembering every time I cried myself to sleep. Remembering every betrayal that cut too deep.

Even till this day, my family makes me feel like no matter what I do, I can't escape the pain. My heart and soul is too heavy, I can't even explain.

I've prayed all the prayers I needed to pray. My hope is slowly fading away.

I'm hoping this pain will be in the past, or I'll be wondering if this pain will kill me and it will be my last.

My Mother and Her High Hopes

Why is it so hard for her to see what I see? How much longer is she still going to believe?

How much more heartbreak and tears does she need? How many more scars till she finally bleeds?

I don't understand why she can't just let it go. The way this family is constantly hurting us like we don't already know.

She thinks we're the same like she feels my pain, but deep down if it were true she would know we're not in the same lane.

I've tried telling her on repeat about how they truly are, the way they'll always cut us deep, deeper than a scar.

I've tried showing her on repeat after constantly making us cry, but even through pain and tears she will always try to deny.

It's like no matter what they do or say, she will always have respect for them and obeys.

But I already did my part, so now it's up to her if she gets her heart completely torn apart.

Change

The girl I used to be was full of hope and light. I remember how it felt to sleep through the night.

The girl I used to be didn't know how pain felt, I wish I could say that now with all that I've dealt.

It's funny how people blame me for how I changed, but don't blame themselves for the reason they broke me, it's kind of strange.

Sometimes it's hard to stay silent when all I want to do is scream. My hurt and anger is combined can't tell which is more extreme.

Yes, I agree I'm not the same. I'm not the little girl smiling in picture frames.

But don't make it seem like I'm in the wrong, from everything I've been through, be glad I made it here strong.

I'm not the same girl I used to be, but I guess that's what pain does so excuse me if the person I am today was always meant to be me.

Behind my Mask

These wounds won't seem to heal. This pain is much too real.

The thoughts never seem to go away, I want to scream but I can't find the words to say.

All this pressure gets way too deep, all these traumas are hard to keep.

How long will this end? How much longer do I have to pretend?

Behind my smile I've been crying from the start, Behind my smile I'm bleeding from my heart.

Maybe one day, I'll be free from this cage, but I guess for right now, I'll be performing on stage.

The Monsters

I still fear the monsters that a child once knew, where the child needs reassurance that monsters aren't real and untrue.

I still quietly open the door so no one can hear, and I still close my eyes shut when the monsters reappear.

I shake when I hear the doorknobs slowly turn, and wait for them to leave but they never learn.

I still shake when I hear their screams. I'm tired of living in fear, and I'm tired of all the schemes.

When will they ever go away? When will they get tired of doing the same things every single day?

But look closely, it's not the monsters that I make it out to be, it's the people who raised me who can't set me free.

The ones who are supposed to love and be a family. are the ones that will never be truly happily.

How Much Longer

I'm tired of carrying all the weight, tired of all the stress and all the worries on my plate.

Tired of the suffering. I feel like there's no air, no matter how much I try to be free, you always make happiness seem so rare.

I try so hard to make things right, but our relationship is so complicated it's not always black and white.

I'm tired of being the bigger person, especially since I shouldn't be. I'm your daughter and you can't even fully open your eyes to see.

How much longer can we go on? How much more tears till they are finally gone?

How much more fighting do we have to do? How much more do you have to put me through?

Instead of always putting me to blame, see right through me and you'll know we will never be the same.

My Voice will Never Matter

You make me feel bad for just being myself, you dismiss my feelings and just leave it on the shelf.

You come to me for someone you rely, but I can't do the same even if I try.

You always pushed me to do something that I don't want to do, and no matter how much I say no it never gets through to you.

You always made me feel trapped in a way, to the point where I can't even leave or even stay.

You always yelled at me for just doing something right by me, and if it weren't for your expectations maybe then it would be clear for you to see.

You always have to be the one in control, but as a mother you failed to manage that role.

And if I ever were to read you what I wrote, you would just call me selfish while I hold back my tears and the lumps in my throat.

But no matter how I try to explain in every way for you to understand, my voice will never measure up to your feelings and demand.

No Matter How Long it Takes

How much more do I need to owe? I'm tired of holding on but can't let go.

Tired of screaming just to be heard, but now I stay silent because that's what they prefer.

They think they know me, but I'm unknown, turns out not only words could turn into stone,

I know I'm strong, but it's so hard to pretend like nothing is wrong.

I blame myself for the brokenness inside, but I blame the world for how I hide.

I'm scared that this overwhelming feeling will never fade, but no matter how long it takes I'll wait whether it's tomorrow or a decade.

Betrayal and Trust

I'm the Type of Person

I'm the type of person who loves more than they deserve. I could take a bullet for them and they just sit back and observe.

I'm the type of person who's going through pain every day, but if anyone needs me I'll be by their sides to stay.

I'm the type of person who will always be there, even if they don't even care.

I'm the type of person who will wipe your tears and hug you tight, even though I suffer when I'm alone at night.

I'm the type of person who prays to God to take all your pain away, even though no one sees me faking a smile every single day.

I'm the type of person who will always put you first, but the real question is would you do the same if it was reversed?

I'm Used to People Leaving

I'm not going to force you to stay in my life. If you want to leave then go ahead just don't stab me with a knife.

Don't tell me you care, when most of the time you're not even there.

Don't smile to my face, then behind my back say I'm a disgrace.

I don't know what it is about me that people always leave. I always give more love than I will ever receive.

So, if you want to leave, there's the door, just don't tell me you care because I've heard it a thousand times before.

The World is Fake

How can people hurt you and yet still act like you're the one to blame? They're the ones who tore the match and wonder why you're burning in flames.

They say they're always there, but in reality they don't even have a heart to care.

Why is it that this world is so fake, to the point where they gave me a heartache?

Why is it the people I would take a bullet for are the ones pulling the trigger? People think I'm doing fine but only God knows that my scars have gotten bigger.

Why do people make promises if, in the end, they were always meant to be broken? So many people cut me deep and left me unspoken.

I will never understand this generation, but I guess real love and real promises are just an imagination.

So, fuck everyone who I thought I could always rely, I never thought a hello could be harder than a goodbye.

But one thing that my heart will always show, even on God himself, I'm the realest person you'll ever know.

Fighting my Battles

Laying awake at night just staring at the ceiling, trying so hard to fight my battles from everything I've been feeling.

So many thoughts run through my mind, wondering why my happiness is so hard to find.

Missing the person I used to be, when I didn't care about anyone's opinions about me.

I'm tired of saying that I'm doing okay, especially when it gets worse every single day.

All I want is someone who's real. Maybe then I'll finally be able to heal.

I apologize to my heart, for the world breaking it and ripping me apart.

It seems like no matter what I do, I will never be good enough for any of you.

Painful Memories

I'm tired of the painful memories that I can't seem to forget. So many people I opened up to and they all left me full of regret.

What happened to the promises and the laughs we shared? I wish you told me straight up so maybe then I could've been prepared.

It's crazy how not a single scar came from an enemy, too bad it was the people most closest that sadly is now just a memory.

If only you all knew how much I loved you, you would be in tears from what you all put me through.

If only you knew how much I prayed, and in the end I'm the one who got played.

But I guess I'm the one to blame, because I mistake their love for a little funny game.

Hopeless

Hopeless is what I'm feeling, want to feel free with everything that I'm dealing,

I'm tired of feeling all this stress and weight on my chest, to the point where my mind cannot rest.

I'm tired of feeling so much anger inside, tired of never forgetting how much tears I've cried,

I guess it's because of my writing that made me feel so deep, or the painful memories that were too real to keep.

I just want to clear my mind and feel some peace, so maybe then my overthinking can finally be released.

Broken Glass

Hoping

Looking at the sky, with thoughts of you and I,

Wishing I knew why, you left me here to cry,

Days are passing by, I still have tears in my eyes,

Hoping you'll reply, and tell me it will be alright.

Did you Ever Really Love Me

I know that you're gone, and I promise I've moved on.

But there is something I need to know, and it's something I can't let go.

Did you ever really love me? Or was I just too blind to see?

Did you ever really care about me? Or am I the only one that thought we were meant to be?

You told me you would always be there, but then the next day you left out of nowhere.

I always thought you were the one that made me heal, but now I can't seem to let go of the thought that your love was never real.

Unspoken

If I speak from my heart I'm afraid it will be broken. If I show you my scars, I'll leave you unspoken.

If you knew my smile wasn't real, you'd judge me for how I really feel.

If you saw how much tears I've cried, you wouldn't even imagine how hard I've tried.

If you knew my pain, you'd be surprised by everything my heart contains.

If you could read my mind, you'd be in tears from what you find.

I'm afraid to show people the real me, so I stay silent and hide my pain so that way they're too blind to ever see.

Hope You're Doing Okay

I don't know why you're still on my mind, it's like no matter how long it's been, I can't leave you behind.

I hope you're doing okay, been thinking about our memories on replay.

I swear I've moved on, but there's something about you that left me so drawn.

I pray to God that he keeps that smile on your face, and I pray that if you're feeling any kind of pain that I would take your place.

I always wanted you to be full of love and laughter, even though you put me through so much pain after.

But never once did I hate you, I put all the pain and tears aside just to make sure your happiness was true.

Loving You

You told me that you loved me, you told me that you cared, if only I knew you only said that just because of a fucking dare.

I don't know why I even try, no matter what, you always made me cry.

I hate how deeply hurt I'm feeling inside, and especially loving you all this time.

I don't know how to let it go, my feelings are still the same even after so long ago.

Lord knows how much my love was real, when it comes to how I really feel.

Worst Fear

Behind my smile there's a hurting heart. Behind my silence I'm falling apart.

No one sees the real me, full of scars and misery.

I try so hard not to lose sight, I've been holding on so tight.

Losing you used to be my fear, now that you're gone I've realized my eyes are finally dry and clear.

Goodbye

The more you overthink, the more it gets deep, the more you listen to the voices in your head, the harder it is for you to fall asleep.

The more you feel, the more it gets real.

The more you believe the lies, the more your heart cries.

The more you love, the harder it gets, I wonder if I'm ever going to forget.

I remember the past, and wish we could've last.

I miss you even though I try to deny, feeling hurt not because you left, but because you never said goodbye.

I See this Girl

There's this girl I see right in front of me, she's trapped in her mind, but she wishes to be free.

She is completely broken and shattered, and she feels like she will never matter.

There's pain behind her smile, and nobody even noticed it's been there for a while,

She's always crying, she's tired of trying.

She says she's okay, but deep down she wants to fade away.

I see that she hates herself, but she stays silent like a book on a shelf.

I kept staring at her and began to see clearer, then I realized…

It was me standing in front of a mirror.

HOME

What is Love

What is love?

Is it pain or is it a cure? Is it the reason behind a heartache or is it a feeling we can feel reassured?

Is it something that leaves you crying at night, or the warmth of being loved that holds you tight?

Is it something that puts a smile on your face, or is it the reason why scars can't be erased?

What is the true meaning of love? Is it something that puts you down or is it a feeling you can rise above?

They say "Love is pain"

… but at the same time, it can also be like a movie kissing underneath rain.

What is the true meaning of love? In my dreams I have hoped that one day I'd know this real and beautiful feeling of.

If I Had to Speak about Love

If I had to speak about love I'd tell them about us. I'll tell the stories of how our relationship is built on trust.

I'll tell them love is something that feels like peace, in a way where all the pain is finally released.

The feeling of a passion so strong, it's a place where you'll know you belong.

I'll tell them a love like that is so rare and so hard to find, when you know it's real love can't be blind.

I'm Falling for You

I never thought I'd feel this way, you make my heart smile without a word to say.

The feeling of your warmth when you hold me tight, and the way I can't stop thinking of you all through the night.

I never thought there would be a day when my heart didn't ache, but because of you, my smile isn't fake.

The way you make me feel is hard to explain, and how you make my heart race is completely insane.

I know I'm not perfect, but you make me feel worth it.

No matter how far we go, my feelings for you will always grow.

Before You

Before you, I never knew what love was, never met someone who liked me even with all my flaws.

Before you, I never felt like anything mattered, but you came and fixed my heart that used to be shattered.

Before you, I had never been treated right, It's because of your love that gets me through the night.

Before you, I never knew a passion could be so strong, but with you, I know that's where I belong.

Before you, I always felt like an outcast, and I know I'm not your first, but I hope I'll be your last.

Before you, I never thought I'd be able to heal, never knew this amazing feeling could be real.

I believe we are meant to be together, because ever since our first kiss I knew you were my today, my tomorrow, and my forever.

You Healed Me

You fixed the broken pieces that you didn't break, you've healed my scars that you didn't even make.

You've dried up my tears when you never made me cry, you've kept me going when I thought I couldn't even try.

You loved a broken heart, and you called me beautiful like I was a piece of art.

You showed me the real true meaning of love, when I believed I was never worthy of.

Didn't think my dream would come true, but I thank my lucky star because it gave me you.

I Love You

Roses are red violets are blue, when we first met I knew my heart would belong to you.

No matter what we do, between thick and thin, I know we will always get it through.

Our love is strong. That's what makes it true, my love for you will never end and that's a promise I'll never break to you.

Happy Valentine's Day

Roses are red violets are blue, my life became better when it's with you.

Valentine's day is about your true love, there's nothing in the world that could be more important or above.

Every day you're my valentine, and every day I celebrate that you are mine.

I love you with every single beat of my heart, and no matter what happens, nothing can ever break us apart.

I Crave you like a Drug

Every time we kiss, my heart begins to melt, every time you're near me, it's a feeling I have never felt.

I love the way your eyes gets locked on mine, and the way I love being with you is something that I can't define.

You make me feel a certain type of way, it's like an addiction I can't stay away.

The way you gently kiss my lips and hold me tight, and the way you say you love my smile that shines so bright.

I don't know what it is that I can't seem to forget, but all I know is that every time your lips are on mine is definitely something I could never regret.

Happy 1 Year Anniversary

12 months, 365 days to make a year, I can't believe we finally made it here.

Every moment of every day, I fall deeper in love with you in every single way,

You have a special place in my heart that no one can ever replace, turns out my home is you and not an actual place.

You've shown me the real true meaning of love, you've given me so much more than I've ever dreamed of.

I want to give you a small thing, that represents my love to you almost like a promise ring.

I promise I'll forever love you, and I promise I'll never stop just know it's true.

Happy 1 year anniversary being together, can't wait to spend the rest of my life with you until forever.

Like a Rose

I didn't realize I'm just like a rose, never understood the thorns that were too exposed.

People took advantage and watched my petals fall, maybe just like the thorns on a rose represents myself building up a wall.

Scared to let anyone in, scared of what they'll take within.

But then you came along and found beauty in my flaws, you looked at every part of my skin and said it's perfection without a doubt or a pause.

Accepted the thorns without looking at the rose, even though a garden full of beautiful flowers I'm the one you chose.

Lust and Desire

The way he makes me feel when he touches me, the way our souls connect like it knows we're meant to be.

I love how he kisses every part of my body that I hate, the way he takes all the pressure off and all the weight.

The way he makes love to me so passionately and full of desire, the way our bodies build heat like the ring of fire.

The way he makes me feel while staring into my eyes, kissing every inch of my skin that gives me chills down to my thighs.

He makes me feel loved in a way I never felt, the power he has over me with one single kiss makes my heart melt.

The best part of us being together, is knowing I'll be his always and forever.

Home

The feeling you make me feel is deeper than the word love, the way you look at me like no one can ever be above.

The way our souls connect like it knows we're meant to be, the way you make my heart smile and only you who has the key.

The way you make me feel safe and secure, who knew our love is the best kind of cure?

Every time I'm with you, my soul feels so complete, and I'm not afraid to let the world know that I love you on repeat.

You are my home, the home I never knew, and as you're reading this now just know I can't wait for the moment where I finally say I do.

Writing Poetry

Writing Poetry

Whether I feel so deep, or my heart has too many scars I can't keep,

I write down what I truly feel inside, I don't write to get attention but ever since I started to write I never had more pride.

My words will always be from the bottom of my heart, and maybe it's not a big deal to others, but to me, it's my piece of art.

My poetry is how I heal, and that's what makes it unique and real.

I don't write what people expect, nor do I write to have fame or respect.

But my poetry is somehow a part of me, and if I want to escape I'll start to write because it makes me express and be free.

I am my own art, and if you want to get to know me, read my poems. It's the best way to know what's real in my heart.

Acknowledgements

I want to thank all the people in my life that made my voice heard and pushed me to publish my book. First, I want to thank everyone on my team who was able to make this beautiful moment happen. Thank you to my close friends that always made my words feel so special. Thank you to all my readers and listeners. I wouldn't have done this without your support. And a special thank you to my most amazing, loving boyfriend that never stopped supporting, motivating, and inspired me to write my book. Thank you for loving me and always making me feel like I am more than enough. I love you, Abiud.

(Always and Forever)

About the Author

Dina Ibrahim's first book of poetry "Break the Silence" is about toxic families, losing friends, experiencing heartbreak, having insecurities, and falling in love. She wrote these topics based on her life. This author is very proud of her words and her writing. She started writing poetry when she was really young and it became a part of her ever since. Dina Ibrahim has wrote this poem reflecting on her life but also wrote this for everyone who has similar traumas, pain, and tears. She hopes that if you do relate to her story, she wanted you to know that you are not alone, and your voice will always matter, even in silence. And to also remind all of you that no matter whose hurt you along the way, just know you deserve better. We deserve to be heard.

www.ingramcontent.com/pod-product-compliance
Lightning Source LLC
LaVergne TN
LVHW051911060526
838200LV00004B/84